The Life and Work of
Leonardo da Vinci

Sean Connolly

Heinemann LIBRARY

www.heinemann.co.uk/library
Visit our website to find out more information about **Heinemann Library** books.

To order:
☎ Phone 44 (0) 1865 888066
🖷 Send a fax to 44 (0) 1865 314091
🖥 Visit the Heinemann Bookshop at www.heinemann.co.uk/library to browse our catalogue and order online.

First published in Great Britain by Heinemann Library, Halley Court, Jordan Hill, Oxford OX2 8EJ, part of Harcourt Education.
Heinemann is a registered trademark of Harcourt Education Ltd.

Editorial: Clare Lewis
Design: Jo Hinton-Malivoire and Q2A Creative
Illustrations by Sally Barton
Production: Helen McCreath

Printed and bound in China by South China Printing Company

10 digit ISBN 0 431 09884 0
13 digit ISBN 978 0 431 09884 5

10 09 08 07 06
10 9 8 7 6 5 4 3 2 1

British Library Cataloguing in Publication Data
Connolly, Sean
The Life and Work of: Leonardo da Vinci - 2nd edition
759.5
A full catalogue record for this book is available from the British Library.

Acknowledgements
The publishers would like to thank the following for permission to reproduce photographs:
Pages 5, 19, Leonardo da Vinci *The Last Supper*, Credit: Giraudon. Page 7, Leonardo da Vinci *The Annunciation*, Credit: Giraudon. Page 8, *Florence, Tuscany, Italy*, Credit: Colorific! Page 9, Leonardo da Vinci *The Baptism of Christ*, Credit: Giraudon. Page 13, Leonardo da Vinci *The Adoration of the Magi*, Credit: Giraudon. Page 15, Leonardo da Vinci *The Virgin of the Rocks*, Credit: Giraudon. Page 16, Leonardo da Vinci *Design for a helicopter*, Credit: AKG. Page 17, Leonardo da Vinci *Sketch for the proposed 'Tiburio' of Milan Cathedral*, Credit: Biblioteca Trivulziana. Page 21, Leonardo da Vinci *Cartoon for the Virgin and child with Saint Anne*, Credit: Giraudon. Page 22, Leonardo da Vinci *Design for assault vehicles*, Credit: AKG. Page 23, Leonardo da Vinci *Sketch to show a technique of pushing down the walls*, Credit: AKG. Page 25, Leonardo da Vinci *Mona Lisa*, Credit: Giraudon. Page 26, Leonardo da Vinci *Studies for a Nativity*, Credit: SCALA. Page 27, Leonardo da Vinci *Saint John the Baptist*, Credit: Giraudon. Page 28, *Chateau Clos Lucé*, Credit: Pix. Page 29, Leonardo da Vinci *Self-Portrait*, Credit: Image Select.

Cover photograph: *Die Dame mit dem Hermilin* by Leonardo da Vinci, reproduced with permission of AKG Images.

The publishers would like to thank Nancy Harris for her assistance in the preparation of this book.

Every effort has been made to contact copyright holders of any material reproduced in this book. Any omissions will be rectified in subsequent printings if notice is given to the publishers.

The paper used to print this book comes from sustainable resources.

Some words in the book are bold, **like this**. You can find out what they mean by looking in the Glossary.

Contents

Who was Leonardo da Vinci?

Leonardo da Vinci was a great painter. He lived in Italy 500 years ago. Leonardo lived at a time when art was becoming important.

Leonardo was also a **sculptor**, a poet, and an **inventor**. He loved nature and science. This painting shows how his pictures looked like real life.

Early years

Leonardo was born on 15 April 1452 in Vinci, Italy. The name "da Vinci" means "from Vinci". When he was young, Leonardo's uncle Francesco taught him about the countryside.

Leonardo never forgot the long walks in
the hills with his uncle. Many years later he
could still paint all the plants he had seen.
He painted some in this picture.

Life in Florence

In 1470 Leonardo went to live in a city called Florence. He learned to paint in the **studio** of Andrea del Verrocchio. Andrea was one of many great painters in Florence.

Andrea painted this picture. Leonardo helped him by painting the angel on the left. Andrea thought the angel was the best part of the painting.

Becoming a master

Leonardo finished his **studies** soon after painting the angel. He could have set up his own **studio**. Instead he stayed in Andrea's house.

In 1474 he painted this **portrait** of a young woman. The dark trees behind her face make her skin look bright.

On his own

Leonardo was 25 years old when he began working for himself. He had learned a lot from Andrea. He had also met many important people.

This unfinished early painting shows us how Leonardo worked. The colours are all shades of brown. Leonardo would have added the brighter colours later.

On to Milan

In 1482 Leonardo went to work for the ruler of the city of Milan. Leonardo lived there with a family of artists called Preda.

Leonardo and the Preda family worked on this painting of Mary with baby Jesus. The lovely mixture of light and dark was the work of Leonardo.

Special skills

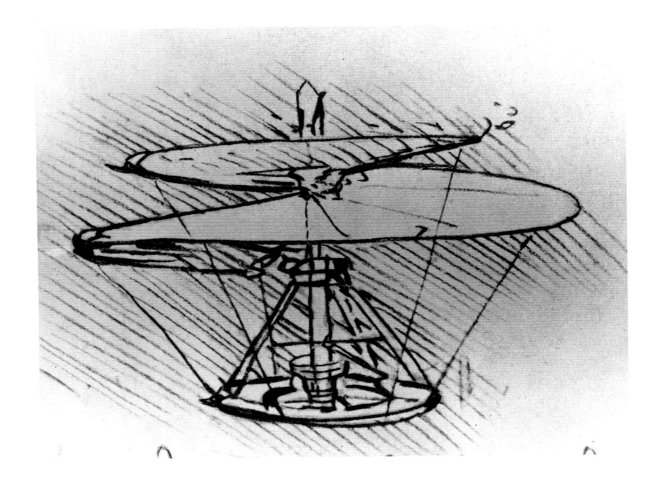

Leonardo **studied** different subjects in Milan. He was very interested in the human body and how water moved. Leonardo also **designed** many things, such as this helicopter.

You can still see many of Leonardo's designs. This **sketch** shows how Leonardo planned to make the **dome** of the great **cathedral** in Milan better.

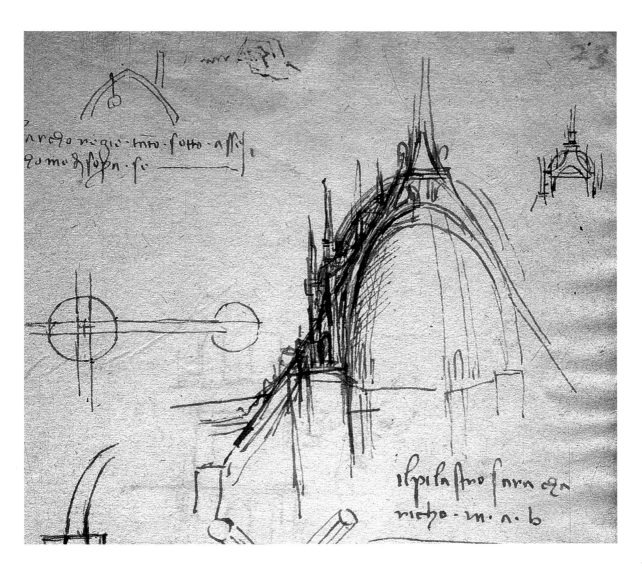

The Last Supper

In 1495 Leonardo began a huge **mural** of Christ's Last Supper. A mural is a picture painted straight on to a wall. Leonardo wanted to show what people are thinking as well as how they look.

The Last Supper shows Christ and his
12 followers, called the **apostles**. The
picture looks like a real supper. It shows
all of the men busy talking and listening.

Florence

In 1499 Milan was attacked. Leonardo escaped and went back to Florence. There he met many other artists.

Other artists liked Leonardo's work. He could show gentle movements and even feelings in his pictures. This **cartoon** shows the Virgin Mary and her mother with Jesus.

New ideas

Leonardo soon had a chance to show his other skills. In 1502 he became the main **military engineer** in central Italy.

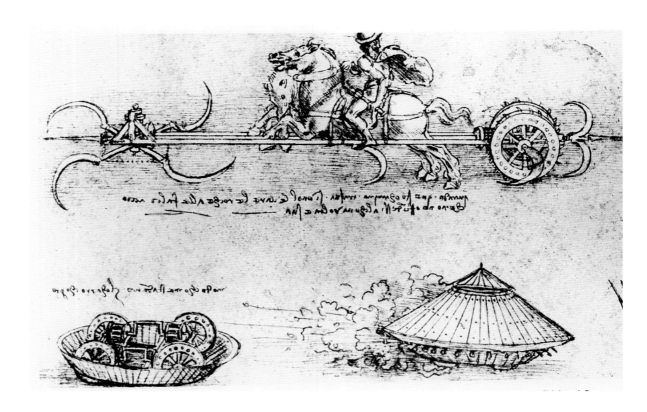

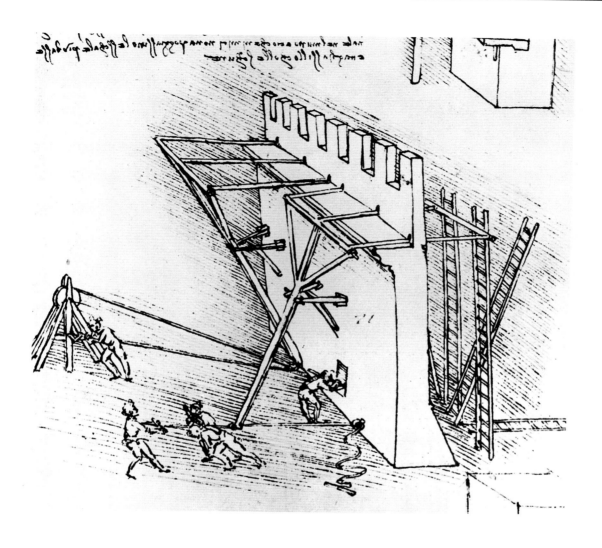

Leonardo drew plans for weapons, **fortresses**, and bridges. This **sketch** of putting up a fortress wall is from a book of his drawings called *Codex Atlanticus*.

The secret smile

Leonardo was very busy but he still found time to work on a special **portrait**. The result was the *Mona Lisa*. This is one of the most famous paintings in the world.

No one can be sure who this woman really was. Her smile has fascinated people for many years. She looks like she is keeping a secret.

With King and Pope

In 1507 Leonardo became painter to a French king who was living in Milan. Seven years later Leonardo moved to Rome as a guest of the **Pope**. This is a **sketch** he made for a painting called *Adoration of the Kings*.

Leonardo's last pictures were **religious**.
The hand of Saint John the Baptist seems
to come right out of this painting.

Last years in France

Leonardo lived as the guest of another French king for his last three years. He made many drawings in his large house in France. He died on 2 May 1519. He was 67 years old.

This **self-portrait** shows Leonardo as an old man. He has lost his teeth and some of his hair. But his eyes are still strong.

Timeline

1452   Leonardo da Vinci is born in Vinci, central Italy on 15 April.

1470   Leonardo moves to Florence and begins training with Andrea del Verrocchio.

1481   Leonardo leaves Andrea's **studio** to work on his own.

1482   Leonardo moves to Milan.

1495   Leonardo begins *The Last Supper*.

1499   Leonardo returns to Florence.

1502   Leonardo becomes **military engineer** in central Italy.

1505–15   Leonardo paints the *Mona Lisa*.

1507   Leonardo moves to Milan as a guest of King Louis XII of France.

1514–16   Leonardo lives in Rome as guest of the **Pope**.

1516   Leonardo moves to France as guest of King François I.

1519   Leonardo dies at Chateau Clos-Lucé, France on 2 May.

Glossary

apostle one of the 12 close friends and followers of Jesus Christ

cartoon quick drawing done before making a painting

cathedral large church, usually in a city

design to think of an idea or plan and put it on paper

dome rounded roof

fortress strong building to guard against enemies

inventor someone who thinks of new ideas for doing or making things

military engineer someone who plans and makes weapons and fortresses

mural picture painted on to a wall

Pope the leader of the Roman Catholic Church

portrait painting of a person

religious to do with what people believe in

sculptor someone who carves wood or stone to make works of art

self-portrait picture that an artist paints of himself or herself

sketch a drawing

studio building or room where an artist works

study learn about a subject

More books to read

Masterpieces: da Vinci, Shelly Swanson Sateren (Franklin Watts, 2004)

The Children's Book of Art, Rosie Dickens (Usborne Publishing, 2005)

More paintings to see

Panels for an Ancona, Leonardo da Vinci, National Gallery, London

The Virgin of the Rocks, Leonardo da Vinci, National Gallery, London

Burlington House Cartoon (Virgin and Child with St Anne), Leonardo da Vinci, National Gallery, London

Index